Spiders

Published by Wildlife Education, Ltd.
12233 Thatcher Court, Poway, California 92064
contact us at: 1-800-477-5034
e-mail at: animals@zoobooks.com
visit us at: www.zoobooks.com

ISBN 0-937934-88-7

Spiders

Series Created by
John Bonnett Wexo

Written by
Timothy Levi Biel

Zoological Consultant
Charles R. Schroeder, D.V.M.
Director Emeritus
San Diego Zoo and San Diego Wild Animal Park

Scientific Consultants
Dr. Herbert W. Levi
Museum of Comparative Zoology,
Harvard University

Dr. Ron Monroe
Entomology Department
San Diego State University

Art Credits

Main Art: Walter Stuart

Pages Eight and Nine: Walter Stuart

Pages Ten and Eleven: Walter Stuart

Page Eleven: Bottom, Jim Melli

Pages Twelve and Thirteen: Walter Stuart

Page Twelve: Bottom, Ed Abrams

Pages Sixteen and Seventeen: Walter Stuart

Page Seventeen: Bottom, Jim Melli

Page Eighteen: Jim Melli

Page Nineteen: Walter Stuart

Page Twenty-Two: Walter Stuart

Page Twenty-Three: Jim Melli

Photographic Credits

Cover: Rod Planck (*Tom Stack & Associates*)

Pages Six and Seven: Adolf Schmidecker (*Alpha/FPG*)

Page Nine: **Top,** William Ferguson; **Middle,** M.P.C. Fogden (*Bruce Coleman, Ltd.*); **Bottom,** Hans Pfletschinger (*Peter Arnold, Inc.*)

Page Ten: Hans Pfletschinger (*Peter Arnold, Inc.*)

Page Eleven: **Top,** Frieder Saver (*Bruce Coleman, Ltd.*); **Bottom,** James P. Rowan (*Click Chicago*)

Page Twelve: Richard Walters

Page Thirteen: Hans Pfletschinger (*Peter Arnold, Inc.*)

Pages Fourteen and Fifteen: Michael Fogden (*Bruce Coleman, Inc.*)

Page Sixteen: Richard K. La Val (*Animals Animals*)

Page Seventeen: **Top,** Stephen Dalton (*Natural History Photos*); **Middle,** Jane Burton (*Bruce Coleman, Inc.*); **Bottom,** Alan Blank (*Bruce Coleman, Inc.*)

Page Eighteen: **Top,** Hans Pfletschinger (*Peter Arnold, Inc.*); **Upper Middle,** Robert Mitchell; **Bottom,** Rod Planck (*Tom Stack & Associates*)

Pages Twenty and Twenty-One: Mik Dakin (*Bruce Coleman, Ltd.*)

Page Twenty-Three: **Top,** Richard Walters; **Bottom,** J.A. Grant (*Natural Science Photos*)

Our Thanks To: Mr. Saul Frommer (*University of California at Riverside*); Michael Kassem; Mike Mitchell, Andy Natonabah, Peggy Scott (*Navajo Community College*); David Faulkner (*San Diego Museum of Natural History*); Melanie Biel; Richard Leonhardt; Tom Clark; Pamela Stuart

Cover Photo: Daddy Longlegs (not a true spider)

Contents

Spiders seldom win popularity contests. When people see spiders, they react in different ways. Some people scream and run away. Others try to kill every spider they see. Some may get out the poison to kill even the spiders they can't see! Occasionally, however, a person will just stop and watch with fascination as a spider spins its web.

Of all possible reactions, this is probably the wisest, because spiders rarely do anything to harm us. Out of thousands of different spiders in the world, only a handful are poisonous to people. The most common poisonous spiders, such as the black widow and the brown recluse, rarely bite people. Far more people die each year from bee and wasp stings than from spider bites.

Spiders are actually useful. They do not harm plants, as some people think. Instead, they protect plants by controlling insects. Spiders are the most important predators of insects in the world. If you see spiders in a garden, it doesn't mean the garden is unhealthy. It means the spiders are helping it stay healthy.

If you take the time to watch spiders, you may be surprised by what you see. There are many wonderful colors, shapes, and sizes of spiders. Some spin beautiful webs. They may perform daring acrobatic feats on their thin, silk threads. Other spiders spin no webs at all. They stalk insects on the ground with all the skill and ferocity of a tiger hunting big game.

Scientists have named about 30,000 species of spiders. But they think this is only one-fourth of all the different spiders in the world. In most species, you can easily tell the female spider from the male because the females are much larger. For example, the female black widow weighs about one hundred times as much as the male.

Female spiders lay eggs. The baby spiders that hatch from these eggs are called spiderlings. After hatching, most spiders live less than a full year, but there are some remarkable exceptions. Tarantulas do not become mature adults until they are 10 or 11 years old. Female tarantulas often live an additional 10 years!

TARANTULA

What is a spider? Many people probably think they know, but they may not be able to tell a spider from other small creatures. Can you? Do you know how many legs spiders have? Do they have wings like an insect or a stinger like a scorpion?

Like insects, spiders are arthropods—they belong to the *phylum* Arthropoda. This is a broad classification that links those animals that have legs with many joints and hard, *external* skeletons that cover their bodies on the outside. This large group also includes shrimps, crabs, lobsters, barnacles, and centipedes. In a narrower classification, spiders, scorpions, mites, and the spider-like daddy longlegs belong to the *class* Arachnida. But a spider is no more closely related to a scorpion than a mouse is to an elephant! So how do you recognize a spider when you see one?

A spider's body has two main parts. The "front" part is called the *cephalothorax*. The spider's eyes, mouth, and stomach are part of the cephalothorax. All spiders have eight legs. The legs are also attached to this part of the body.

CEPHALOTHORAX

FANGS

JAWS

PEDIPALPS

The spider's mouth has two large *jaws*. At the tip of each jaw is a sharp, curved *fang*. Alongside each jaw is a *pedipalp*. Pedipalps are used like feelers so the spider can sense what is around it. They are also used to hold prey down while the spider bites it with its fangs.

8 LEGS

JUMPING SPIDER

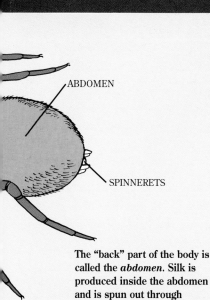

ABDOMEN

SPINNERETS

The "back" part of the body is called the *abdomen*. Silk is produced inside the abdomen and is spun out through *spinnerets* located at the end of the abdomen.

IS THIS A SPIDER?

The crane fly has long legs like a spider. But it only has *six legs*. That's because crane flies are insects, not spiders. You can also tell that this is not a spider, because it has *wings*. Spiders do not have wings.

IS THIS A SPIDER?

Scorpions have eight legs and a pair of pedipalps, just like spiders. But a scorpion's pedipalps are huge *pincers*. And its long, thin body is divided into several segments, not just two. Also, the scorpion's "tail" end has a *stinger*. All these things make scorpions different from spiders.

IS THIS A SPIDER?

Mites are so tiny they look like walking specks of dust. But magnified, like the velvet mite below, they look like spiders. If you look carefully, you will see that the mite's *body* is not divided into two parts the way a spider's is. Instead, it is all one piece with no separation between the head and the abdomen.

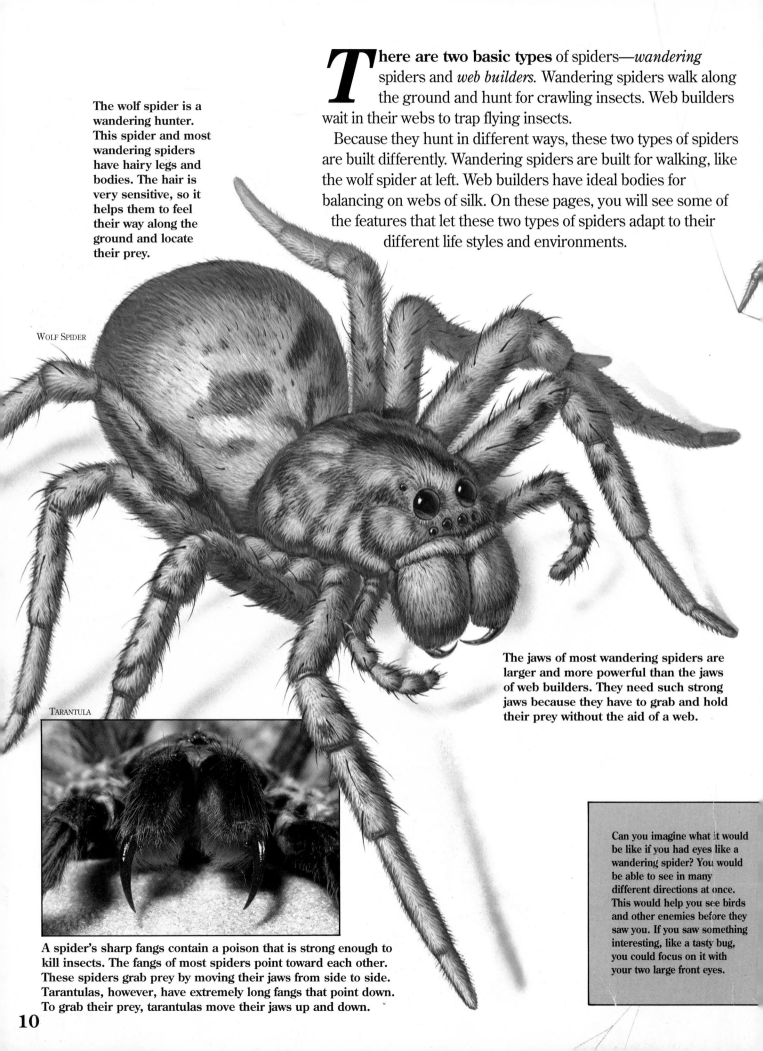

The wolf spider is a wandering hunter. This spider and most wandering spiders have hairy legs and bodies. The hair is very sensitive, so it helps them to feel their way along the ground and locate their prey.

There are two basic types of spiders—*wandering* spiders and *web builders.* Wandering spiders walk along the ground and hunt for crawling insects. Web builders wait in their webs to trap flying insects.

Because they hunt in different ways, these two types of spiders are built differently. Wandering spiders are built for walking, like the wolf spider at left. Web builders have ideal bodies for balancing on webs of silk. On these pages, you will see some of the features that let these two types of spiders adapt to their different life styles and environments.

WOLF SPIDER

TARANTULA

The jaws of most wandering spiders are larger and more powerful than the jaws of web builders. They need such strong jaws because they have to grab and hold their prey without the aid of a web.

A spider's sharp fangs contain a poison that is strong enough to kill insects. The fangs of most spiders point toward each other. These spiders grab prey by moving their jaws from side to side. Tarantulas, however, have extremely long fangs that point down. To grab their prey, tarantulas move their jaws up and down.

Can you imagine what it would be like if you had eyes like a wandering spider? You would be able to see in many different directions at once. This would help you see birds and other enemies before they saw you. If you saw something interesting, like a tasty bug, you could focus on it with your two large front eyes.

Web builders use their long, skinny legs to perform daring "high wire acts." With eight long legs to help them balance, they seem to dance and glide over their webs.

RED WIDOW

Although all spiders can spin silk, the real experts are the web builders. They usually have three or four pairs of spinnerets that spin different textures of silk to do different jobs.

These spiders can spin anything from thin strands, as shown above, to thick sheets of silk. They can make their silk as sticky as glue or as slippery as ice.

Web-building spiders have tiny eyes and poor eyesight. They rely on their sense of touch more than their vision. Their sensitive legs can feel every little vibration on their webs. That is how they locate their prey.

The feet of a web builder are different from those of a wandering spider. Wandering spiders have *two claws* on each foot. Between the claws is a pad of hair **1**. This gives them a firm grip for walking on slippery surfaces. Web builders have *three claws* on each foot **2**. The middle claw hooks over the silk threads of their webs.

WOLF SPIDER

1

A wandering spider needs good eyesight to see where it's going, to be safe from predators, and to find food. When the wolf spider is ready to attack its prey, it focuses on the prey with its two huge front eyes.

2

Web-building spiders use silk to build shelters, catch prey, and move from place to place. For these things, a spider must have different kinds of silk. Fortunately, most spiders can make their silk thick or thin, weak or strong, slippery or sticky, or just about any way they need it.

There are many different kinds of web-building spiders, and they build different kinds of webs. Some webs look very beautiful, while others just look like a tangle of threads. But every web is just right for its builder. You can even tell by the shape of the web what kind of spider built it. Can you find an *orb weaver*, a *triangle spider*, a *funnel weaver*, a *cobweb weaver*, a *"net thrower,"* and a *water spider* on these pages by looking at their webs?

Most web builders wrap their prey with sticky silk before they bite it. This prevents the prey from kicking its way free, or from stinging to defend itself. Also, once its food is wrapped, the spider doesn't have to eat until it gets hungry.

AN ORB WEAVER builds a web shaped like an orb, or circle. Day or night, its web is almost invisible. Some orb weavers sit in the center of their webs and wait for insects to fly into them. Others, like the shamrock spider (at right) hide alongside the web until they feel it vibrating. Then they know they have caught something, and they rush out to attack it.

A FUNNEL WEAVER builds a funnel-shaped web in the grass. This spider hides in the small end of the funnel, where it waits for insects to land on its web. Then it rushes out from its hiding place and grabs them.

Purse-web spiders make tubes for webs and build them alongside tree trunks. They mix dirt with their silk to make the tube look like part of the tree. Then they spend most of their lives inside the tube waiting for insects to come by, like the grasshopper at right *1*.

1   *2*

In a flash, the spider thrusts its fangs through the silk wall of the tube, grabs its prey, and pulls it inside *2*.

Some spiders use their silk in unusual ways. The bolas spider makes a remarkable weapon similar to that used by South American gauchos! This spider spins a ball of sticky silk on the end of a strong silken thread. The bolas spider is able to attract male moths by imitating the smell of a female moth. When the moth approaches, the spider hits it with its gooey ball of silk. The moth sticks to the ball, and the spider pulls in its line.

TRIANGLE SPIDERS weave webs shaped like triangles. This is one of the cleverest traps for snaring flies and other insects. The spider waits beside its web while holding on to a single line of silk. When an insect hits the web, the triangle spider shakes its line. This tangles the insect in the web and it can't get away.

There is nothing more fascinating than watching a spider build its web. An orb weaver builds a frame for its web with spokes going out from the center like the spokes on a bicycle wheel. The spider then weaves its round web onto this frame.

A "NET THROWER" is a special kind of cobweb weaver. Its real name is the ogre-faced spider. Unlike most web spiders, it doesn't just wait for insects to land on its web. Instead, it spins a small rectangular net that it holds as it hangs upside down to wait for ants and other unsuspecting insects to crawl by. When they do, it throws its net over them.

COBWEB WEAVERS have special "teeth" on their back legs to comb their silk. This makes the silk look soft and fluffy. It also makes tiny loops in the silk that can trip insects and entangle them. The black widow is a cobweb weaver that produces some of the strongest silk in the world. As you see below, its web looks like a tangled mess.

THE WATER SPIDER builds a web underwater that looks like a dome. To build this web, the water spider fastens thick sheets of silk to underwater plants. Then it carries air bubbles from the surface to fill its dome with air. This spider can feed, mate, and raise a family inside its airy web.

13

A hunting spider in the Costa Rican
rain forest carries its egg cocoon.

Wandering spiders do not build webs. They live on the ground, in burrows, under rocks, inside tree hollows, and in other protected places. Most of them are active hunters because they cannot just sit and wait for prey to come to them. Instead, wandering spiders must go looking for food.

There are many different kinds of wandering spiders, and they hunt in different ways. Many are like tigers that stalk prey along the ground before leaping on them. Some climb trees, and others dig burrows to hide from their prey. There are spiders that "fish" for prey, and there is even one that catches insects by *spitting* on them! Insects are the main food of all these spiders, but you may be surprised to see the other things that some of them catch.

TARANTULA

Some tarantulas capture small tree frogs. Tarantulas are good at climbing trees. They have pads of sticky hair on the bottoms of their feet that help them climb on slippery leaves and branches, where they can find tree frogs.

Most spiders are afraid of birds, but the bird-eating spiders of South America stalk small birds. These tarantulas may get as big as hummingbirds. Sometimes they even try to sneak up on hummingbirds and drag them from their nests! However, if a hummingbird sees one of these spiders coming, it usually flies away before the spider can catch it.

To catch prey, jumping spiders often leap more than 50 times their body length. If you could jump as well as a jumping spider, you could leap from one end of a football field to the other in a single bound!

JUMPING SPIDER

FISHING SPIDER

Jumping spiders not only jump a long way, they also jump very accurately. A jumping spider usually stalks an insect until it is about a foot away. Then the spider takes a giant leap and lands right on its prey.

This wandering spider goes fishing for most of its food. It can run across the surface of the water and grab insects that have landed or fallen on the water. It can also dive beneath the surface to catch water bugs and even small fish, as you see above.

TRAPDOOR SPIDER

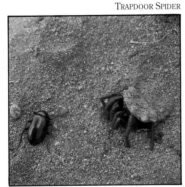

The spitting spider traps insects by spitting on them! It spits a sticky glue from its fangs. This keeps the prey stuck to the ground so it cannot escape.

A trapdoor spider is a wandering spider that doesn't wander. Instead, it hides in a burrow to ambush prey. This spider lines its burrow with silk and covers it with a "trapdoor." Inside, the spider waits until it feels the vibration of an insect passing by. Then it pops out and captures it.

17

Baby spiders grow up quickly. In fact, the entire life of a spider may be less than one year long. Many spiderlings hatch in the spring from eggs laid the summer before. Others hatch in the fall and live through the winter.

For the first few days of life, most spiderlings live with other newly hatched spiders. But eventually, every spider must begin to look for food. In order to spread out and find places to hunt or build their webs, young spiders have a special way of traveling through the air, called *ballooning*.

Only a small number of ballooning spiders lands safely and finds enough food to survive. Those that do usually become adults by late summer. Then they are ready to mate. Shortly after mating, most male spiders die. But females live longer so they can lay their eggs. Some mother spiders even live long enough to guard their eggs and protect the young after they hatch. One typical spider that does this is the wolf spider, shown below.

Spiders begin life as tiny eggs in an egg sac. The number of eggs varies from species to species. Often there are more than a hundred eggs in a single egg sac.

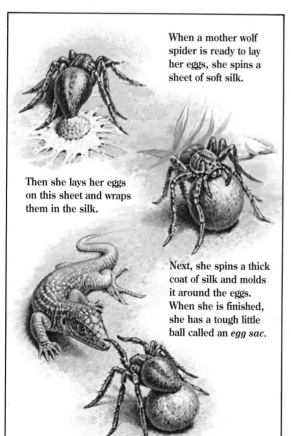

When a mother wolf spider is ready to lay her eggs, she spins a sheet of soft silk.

Then she lays her eggs on this sheet and wraps them in the silk.

Next, she spins a thick coat of silk and molds it around the eggs. When she is finished, she has a tough little ball called an *egg sac*.

The mother keeps her egg sac close to her. She guards it from lizards and other small predators.

When it first hatches, a spiderling remains in the egg sac. Its tiny body is not completely formed, and it cannot see or move.

NURSERY WEB SPIDERS

After a few days, the spiderlings are big enough to climb out of the egg sac. In some species, these newly hatched spiders work together to build a web. This is called a *nursery web*. The young spiders stay on the nursery web until they get hungry. Then they set out to find places of their own.

After her babies hatch, a mother wolf spider has an unusual way of looking after them. She carries them on her back wherever she goes. For several days, she may carry hundreds of little spiderlings this way.

FEMALE WOLF SPIDER AND YOUNG

18

When it reaches the top, the spiderling lets out a few thin threads of silk, which it keeps attached to its abdomen.

As the breeze catches these threads, it lifts the spiderling right into the air. Soon the spiderling is sailing along in the wind. Young spiders sometimes travel hundreds of miles this way!

When spiderlings are ready to look for food and places to live, they often balloon through the air. To do this, a spiderling must climb to the top of a branch or a blade of grass.

The hard skin on the outside of a spider's body is actually its skeleton. In order to grow, the spider must shed its skeleton. When the skeleton splits open, the spider slips out already wearing a new skeleton that will stretch to fit as it hardens. A wolf spider, like the one above, sheds about 12 times before it is completely grown. Each time it sheds, it leaves the old skeleton hanging behind.

19

The ancient Greeks believed that a woman named *Arachne* was the ancestor of all spiders. Scientists often refer to spiders as *arachnids*, and have given the name *Arachnida* to the class of animals that includes spiders. Arachne's story was often told in pictures such as this.

Arachne was a weaver. Her weavings were the most beautiful in all of Greece. But Arachne had one fault—she was very proud. She even claimed that she could weave better than the Greek goddess Athena. This made the goddess so angry that she turned Arachne into a tiny spider. The cloth that Arachne wove became her web.

People have mixed feelings about spiders. On the one hand, they are often afraid of spiders. But on the other hand, they are also fascinated by them. When people fear spiders, it's usually because they do not know much about them. As they learn more about spiders, they become more fascinated and less frightened.

In ancient times, people lived closer to nature and often created myths and legends about the animals they saw, including spiders. Today, we still enjoy telling these old tales. By listening to the legends and learning about spiders, we can discover how interesting they are. And if we follow a few safety rules, we can learn a lot about spiders just by watching them in our yards, parks, and playgrounds.

People may have learned to weave by watching spiders. At least that is what the Navajo people once believed. According to an ancient Navajo legend, a young girl wandered away from her village one day. When the girl found a big hole in the ground, she peeked inside.

To her great surprise, the young girl had discovered the underground home of the Spider Woman, who sat at her loom weaving a beautiful blanket. The Spider Woman welcomed the girl, who stayed with her for several days and learned the secrets of weaving. When the girl returned to her people, she taught them everything the Spider Woman had shown her. To this day, the Navajos are known for their beautifully woven blankets.

Only a few species of spiders are poisonous to humans. For your own safety, you should learn to recognize such common poisonous spiders as the black widow (below) and the brown recluse (right). The brown recluse is common in the southern and western United States. It is brown, it has six eyes, and it has a mark on the top of its cephalothorax that looks like a violin. Can you find the violin?

BROWN RECLUSE

BLACK WIDOW

Spiders do not go looking for people to bite. In fact, they try to stay out of people's way. But you may find them in unswept corners of houses, barns, and garages, because these are good places to build webs. If you sweep the corners regularly, spiders will not stay there.

In the United States and southern Canada, there are a variety of black widows with a variety of markings. But the warning mark to be aware of on this shiny, usually black spider is bright red and is shaped like an hourglass. This identifying mark appears on the *underside* of the round abdomen. Black widows of *every* variety have this mark.

TO BE SAFE, always follow the rules below.

RULE 1: Do not touch a spider if you aren't sure what kind it is.

RULE 2: If you happen to get bitten by a spider, catch it with a jar so it can be identified, if necessary.

You can learn about spiders by watching them. And you can find them just about anywhere. If you search for them, you may find web-building spiders repairing their webs or making new ones. You may see them catching or tying up insects. Look beside rocks, and you may find wolf spiders and jumping spiders hunting for prey.

If you keep an eye on the same web for several days, you will see some interesting changes. One day you may see two spiders on the same web — a big female and a much smaller male. A few days later, you could see a female carrying her egg sac fastened to her abdomen. And someday, you may even find a webful of baby spiders.

You can collect spider webs without harming spiders. To do this, you need a can of spray lacquer, a pair of scissors, and a supply of sturdy black paper.

First, spray the web (without the spider) with three or four *light coats of lacquer* **1**. When the lacquer dries, place a piece of paper behind the web. Then cut the web free and catch it on your paper **2**. Spray the web with a final coat of lacquer so it will stick to the paper **3**.

Index